ROBOZONES

ROBOT WORKERS

DAVID JEFFERIS

Crabtree Publishing Company
www.crabtreebooks.com

INTRODUCTION

Robot workers are machines that work on their own, or are controlled by humans. They help to get jobs done in factories, offices, and people's homes.

The first robot workers were developed in the early 1960s and were used in factories.

The science of robotics has developed quickly. Today, robots do thousands of different jobs, including building cars and cleaning homes.

Crabtree Publishing Company
www.crabtreebooks.com

PMB 16A
350 Fifth Ave.
Ste. 3308
New York

616 Welland Ave
St. Catharines, ON
Canada
L2M 5V6

Edited by
Isabella McIntyre

Coordinating editor
Ellen Rodger

Editors
Rachel Eagen, Carrie Gleason,
Adrianna Morganelli, L. Michelle Nielsen

Production coordinator
Rose Gowsell

Educational advisor
Julie Stapleton

Technical consultant
Mat Irvine FBIS

Created and produced by
David Jefferis/Buzz Books

©2007 David Jefferis/Buzz Books

Library and Archives Canada Cataloguing
in Publication

Jefferis, David
    Robot workers / David Jefferis.

(Robozones)
Includes index.
ISBN-13: 978-0-7787-2885-6 (bound)
ISBN-10: 0-7787-2885-4 (bound)
ISBN-13: 978-0-7787-2899-3 (pbk.)
ISBN-10: 0-7787-2899-4 (pbk.)
    1. Robots--Juvenile literature. 2.
Robots, Industrial--Juvenile
literature. I. Title. II. Series.

TJ211.2.J434 2006
j629.8'92
                        C2006-904120-2

Library and Archives Canada Cataloguing
in Publication

Jefferis, David.
    Robot workers / by David Jefferis.
        p. cm. -- (Robozones)
    Includes index.
    ISBN-13: 978-0-7787-2885-6 (rlb)
    ISBN-10: 0-7787-2885-4 (rlb)
    ISBN-13: 978-0-7787-2899-3 (pbk)
    ISBN-10: 0-7787-2899-4 (pbk)
    1. Robots--Juvenile literature. 2. Robots,
Industrial--Juvenile literature. I. Title.
    TJ211.2.J456 2006
    629.8'92--dc22
                        2006020229

Pictures on these pages, clockwise from left:
1 The Care-O-bot was designed to work as a household assistant.
2 Welding robots working on Mini cars.
3 The Shadow Hand is a highly advanced robotic hand. Its fingers are sensitive enough to detect a small coin.
4 This robotic vacuum cleaner, called the Roboking, is made by LG.

Previous page shows:
Guide and information robots working in a vehicle show room.

CONTENTS

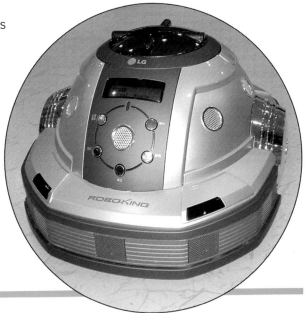

MARCH OF THE MACHINES

Industrial robots are robot workers that make goods, such as cars, often in factories. The first industrial robots were made by the American company, Unimation. Today, robots are essential in many factories.

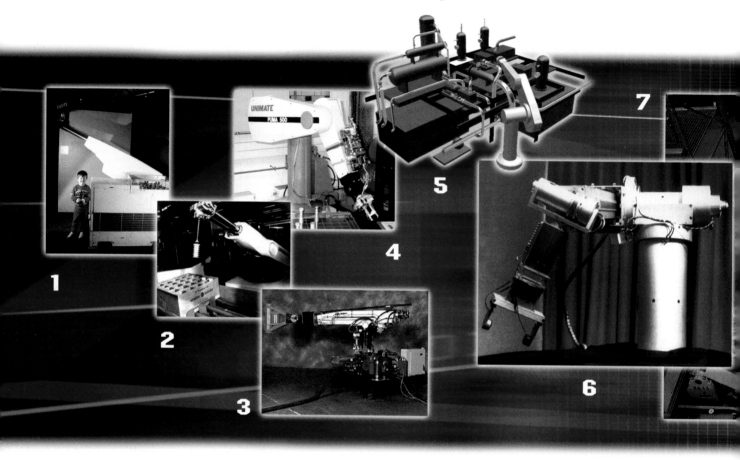

▲ Early robots include:
1, 2, 3 Three of the early industrial robots built by Unimation.
4, 5 PUMA, or Programmable Universal Machine for Assembly, is an industrial robot arm used in factories and research laboratories that became popular during the 1970s.
6 The Stanford Arm, built in 1969, was the first industrial robot with an arm that moved smoothly in three dimensions. The design for PUMA robots was based on the Stanford Arm.

The first industrial robot was called the Unimate. It was dreamt up in 1956 by two inventors, George Devol and Joseph Engelberger. Devol and Engelberger used robots that had appeared in science fiction stories to inspire their designs. In 1961, after five years of development, the first Unimate joined the assembly line at a General Motors automobile plant.

This first Unimate was a "pick and place" machine. It picked up and stacked hot pieces of metal. The 4,000-pound (1,815-kilogram), one-armed robot performed tasks by following a list of step-by-step instructions that were stored on a magnetic drum, an old form of computer memory. Today, Unimates are among the most widely used industrial robots.

▼ Further progress with robot workers includes:
7 Welding **robots** work in many factories across the world.
8 This milling gantry, or metal-shaping robot, has five heads, allowing it to work quickly.
9 The P3 robot is one of several robots developed since 1986 by Honda of Japan.
10 The KUKA Robocoaster moves its riders in all directions.
11 The Kokoro Actroid receptionist robot understands and speaks four languages.

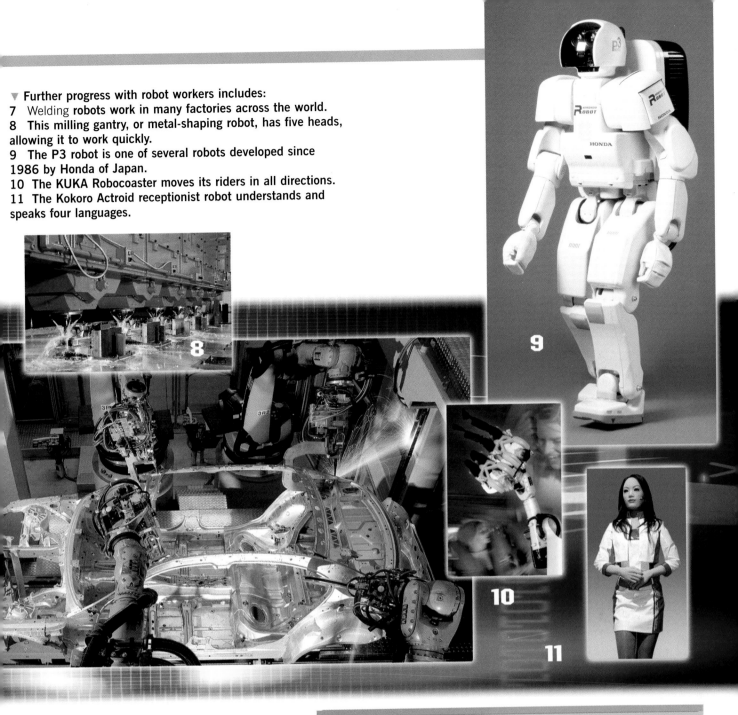

There are many advantages to using robots to make things. They are very accurate, and do not get tired. Robots do not eat lunch, take holidays, or get sick. Like all machines, however, they need to be checked over to make sure they are in good working order, and must be fixed if they break down.

Many robots can change jobs. For example, when a new car design comes out, robots are reprogrammed with new instructions.

ROBOFACTS: MICROCHIP BRAIN

The secret of success for any robot lies in its computer microchip or "brain," a tiny electronic device that processes information and controls what the robot does.

Microchips send instruction to other parts of the robot over circuits. Circuits are electronic paths that carry information between two parts of a machine.

A microchip and its many electronic connections

ANATOMY OF AN ARM

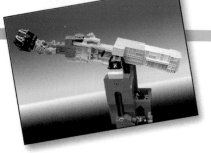

▲ This working robot arm was made with hundreds of plastic Lego construction blocks.

Robots made for different jobs often have similar mechanical parts. Most industrial robots are equipped with one or more mechanical arms.

The first industrial robots consisted of an arm and gripper, or a part that grabs and holds onto objects, linked to a control box. This is still the most popular design for robots in factories.

Robot arms come in many different lengths and may have more than one elbow joint. They are controlled by a complex system of **rams**, pulleys, and switches.

▲ The Mitsubishi company of Japan is a top robot maker. Here, the robot's grippers are holding a tangerine, showing that the arm can handle objects gently, despite its size.

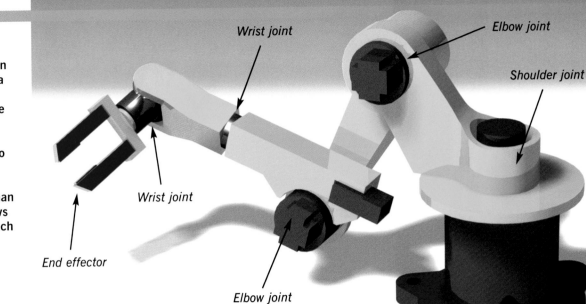

Wrist joint

Elbow joint

Shoulder joint

Wrist joint

End effector

Elbow joint

▶ Unlike human arms, those of a robot can be made with more than one joint. This model has two elbows, two wrists, and a shoulder joint. Having more than two joints allows the arms to reach more areas, or workspace.

Cables and wires are covered with protective casing so they do not get damaged.

A robot arm's movements are measured by the number of ways it can twist, turn, or roll. This is called DOF, or degrees of freedom. A human arm's movements can also be measured using DOF. An elbow has two degrees of freedom, up and down, while a wrist has six, because it can also twist and turn. The movements of a shoulder increases an arm's overall DOF.

▲ The "end effector" is at the tip of a robot's arm. Unlike human fingers, the end effector is designed to suit the job a robot does. There are many different end effectors, including grippers that hold on to things, welding guns to weld parts, paint sprayers that paint, and suction pads that grab onto things.

ROBOFACTS: AN ARM IN SPACE

A Canadian-made robot arm is being used by American space shuttles to handle cargoes in space.

The Remote Manipulator System, or RMS, arm is 50 feet (15 meters) long and has six joints along its length. In the weightless conditions of space, the arm can move objects of up to 32 tons (29 tonnes), such as cargoes, satellites, and space telescopes.

Back on Earth, the effect of gravity means the arm cannot even move its own weight!

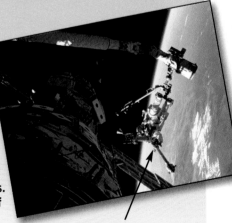

On Earth, the RMS arm weighs 905 pounds (410 kilograms)

PRECISION WORKERS

Industrial robots come in many shapes and sizes. While different industrial robots do different jobs, they are all able to perform very precise tasks.

Industrial robots are able to do their jobs with more accuracy than humans. Some robots are built to lift heavy loads and can move their load quickly back and forth to an accuracy of 0.004 inches (0.1 millimeters). Robots designed for extra-precise work, such as those used in medical research or computer manufacturing, are even more exact than this.

▲ The arms of the K-1207i can reach out 50 inches (1.3 meters) while holding a load weighing up to 35 pounds (16 kilograms).

◄ The Alio robot can place objects to an accuracy much finer than the width of a human hair.

Not all robots have arms that move like human arms. In fact, Scara, or Selective Compliance Articulated Robot Arm, robots usually have two or three swivelling joints, which allow them to move horizontally. They move up and down by sliding along a column.

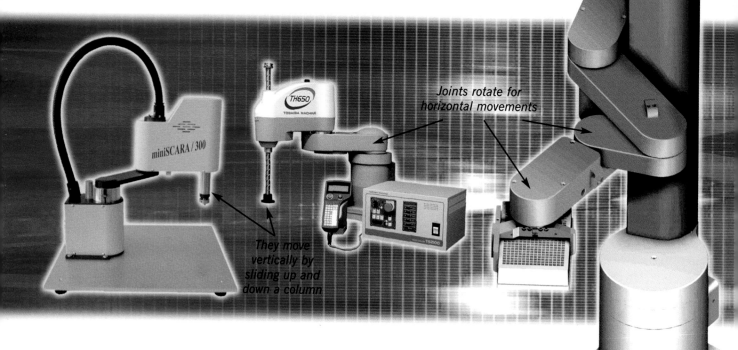

Joints rotate for horizontal movements

They move vertically by sliding up and down a column

▲ Scara robots are industrial robots common around the world.

▲ A medical robot speeds up a research project by working at a nonstop pace picking and placing trays of bacteria.

ROBOFACTS: ROBOTS REPLACING OUR LIMBS?

The earliest artificial limbs were used more than 2,000 years ago by the Romans to replace arms and legs lost in battle.

Until recently, artificial limbs were heavy and difficult to use. Today, researchers are working on robot limbs that move more like human limbs. The movements of this experimental robot hand, pictured at right, are adjusted precisely by a tiny micro-computer. The robot hand can detect if the fingers are slipping off an object. It instantly tightens its grip before the object is dropped.

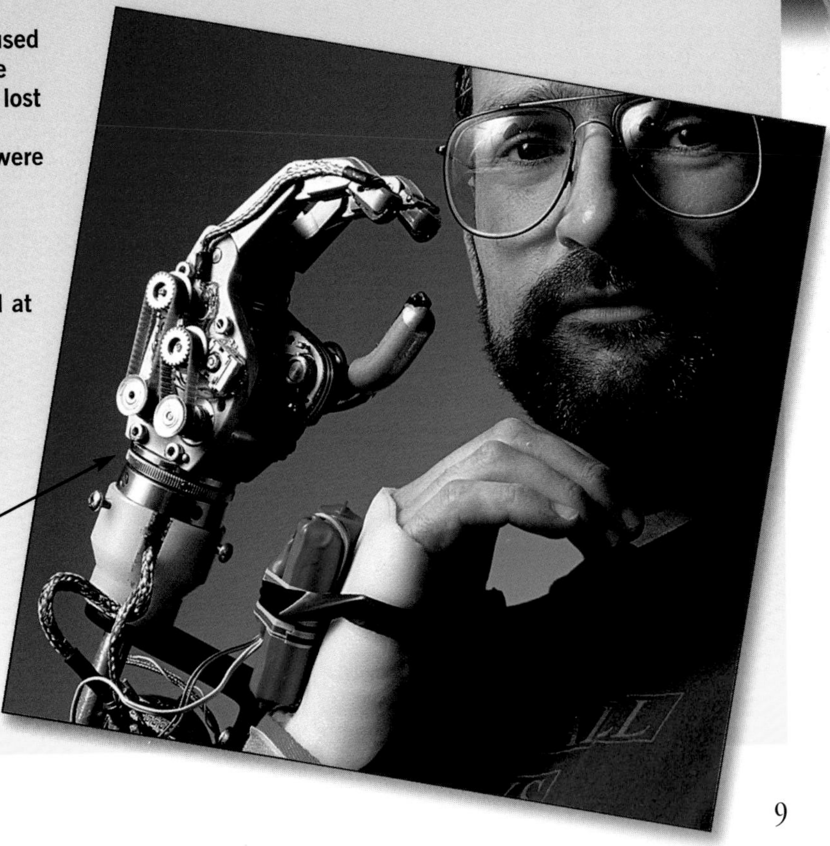

The metal structure of the hand can be covered with plastic "flesh"

▲ A recent Unimate robot.

MILLIONS OF ROBOTS

The number of industrial robot workers continues to grow. In less than 50 years, the world has gone from having a few dozen to having millions.

▲ Robots in this car plant include ones that place roofs (1) and assemble engine parts (2).

Industrial robots have been so successful that their numbers have risen dramatically. In 1961, there were only a few, but 20 years later more than 80,000 robot workers were hard at work. Today, there are more than a million industrial robots in factories all over the world.

In the early days of robotics, people thought robots might take over all jobs. That has not happened. Today, humans and robots are often mixed together, working in teams. There are many different kinds of robots. Robots with a single arm have been joined by robots with several arms. While many robots stay in one spot, others move around a factory on wheels or tracks.

◀ Welding robots were among the first industrial robots. Their work is far more accurate and reliable than that of human welders.

► Robot workers enable vehicles and other products to be made extremely accurately. In an automated car plant, even big parts like doors are assembled to an accuracy of less than 0.04 inches (one millimeter).

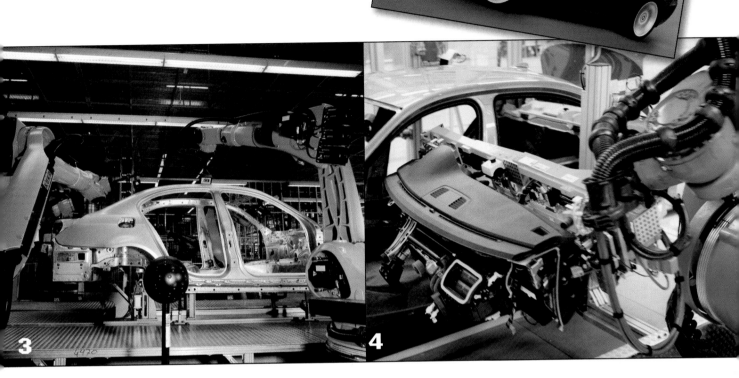

▲ Robots measure a car's body (3) and an instrument panel is inserted through a doorless body (4).

Vehicle assembly plants were among the first factories to use robots. In many vehicle plants, cars are put together on an assembly line, which is a slow-moving track where vehicles are assembled, part by part.

At the start, the only part on the line is the vehicle base, or floor pan. Welding robots join the body to the floor pan, then various other parts are added, including the engine, gearbox, doors, seats, and wheels. At some points along the line, groups of robots can be seen building and attaching parts, while other parts are still installed by people.

ROBOFACTS: SENSORS

Sensors are a robot's electronic senses, or the way it detects the world. Sensors work much like our own human senses of sight, hearing, smell, taste, and touch. Electronic sensors include such items as cameras for seeing and microphones for hearing.

Few robots need more than one or two senses, and even then they often only need to detect a specific thing. For example, an industrial robot's vision may need to detect only an object's shape. In this case, a simple camera system would do the job.

Video cameras are a robot's "eyes"

DOWN ON THE FARM

▲ High-tech farming in the late 1800s consisted of big steam-powered machines, which helped large teams of humans.

Farming was once done almost entirely by hand. Then, machines, such as tractors, replaced many workers. Today, robots are taking things a step further.

Robots are showing up on farms. They could change the way people cultivate and harvest food crops. Researchers are working on various robotic systems that will vastly reduce the number of human workers farmers will need, saving them the cost of labor. The robotic harvester shown below can be controlled by a person or can be switched to "robot mode."

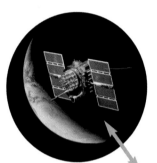

▲ ▶ A GPS satellite sends precise map information to an antenna on the harvester, and is accurate to within three feet (one meter).

▶ The picture at top right shows a robot's eye view of a track. It is not as sharp as the human eye, but is accurate enough for steering.

Steering controls allow a person to operate the harvester

A robot tractor makes a turn

▼ An antenna checks the ground ahead for rough and smooth areas. The information is sent to the computer in charge of steering.

▼ ▶ Robotic farm equipment includes:

1,2   Experimental robot lawn mowers.
3,4,5 Robots built to load and place potted plants.
6,7,8 Ransomes Spider is already on sale as a remote-controlled mower. The robot version can work by itself, running off a computer program.
9   Experimental walking robot will be useful for working on ground too rough for wheels.

Mowing even a small lawn is a time-consuming chore. For people with a lot of grass to cut, such as farmers or golf course owners, it is also very expensive, since people are often hired to operate the equipment.

The Spider, a remote-controlled lawn mower, could be the answer. An experimental version has been fitted with a computer and sensors, which makes it a robot that can work on its own, or with others in a team.

ROBOFACTS: LOOKING BY LASER

Most robots use video cameras as "eyes," but there are other kinds of vision. The picture (right) shows the view seen by a ladar, or LAser Detection And Ranging, system, which uses a pencil-thin laser light beam to scan the landscape. An antenna picks up flashes of laser light that reflect back from objects caught by the beam.

The system then uses a computer pattern-recognition program to determine what the various shapes are and if the robot should avoid them.

Trees

Person walking

Bushes

ROBOTS IN STORE

▲ This robot musician plays in stores for shoppers.

Robots and other computer systems are helping to make working and shopping in stores quicker and easier.

▲ Oskar was designed to lead people around a car showroom. Oskar works up to ten hours before its batteries need to be recharged.

Oskar and Mona, the grey and orange robots on this page, were designed to give people information. They were tested in the showrooms of a German car company. Their jobs were to guide shoppers around, communicating with them using video screens on their chests. Research shows that many shoppers actually like the help of a machine, rather than a salesperson.

Robots also help to ship products from factories, where they are made, to warehouses, which store the products, and shops, where they are purchased. Powerful computers track customer orders. Robots that work in factories can also pack, seal, and load finished products aboard trucks or other transport vehicles, ready for delivery to a warehouse or directly to the customer.

▶ Both Mona and Oskar use laser scanners to sense their environments. They move around on wheels powered by an electric motor. The wheels are hidden by the safety bumper at the base.

ROBOFACTS: RADIO TAGS FOR AUTOMATED SHOPPING

RFID (Radio Frequency IDentification) allows a store's central computer to check inventory, or the number of products a store has. RFID "tags" (right) with a built-in computer chip and radio antenna are attached to items on sale. The central computer and its robotic warehouse assistants track RFID items as they are sold, making sure stock is replaced as needed.

Antenna

Computer chip

Prices on RFID tags can be changed instantly, so slow-sellers can be changed to sale-price bargains

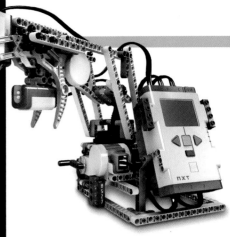

▲ ◀ A robot packing machine seals a box of Lego building block kits before it is sent out on delivery. The picture above shows a robotic arm made of Lego.

The ABB company is one of the world's biggest industrial robot makers. ABB robots are designed to help companies get their products to customers quickly. The robot shown on the left packs boxes so they are ready to ship to stores and other customers.

An automated shopping assistant displays products and guides shoppers around a store

Scanner reads items in cart

When a store runs out of an item, it can be ordered instantly from a warehouse robot

ROBOT CLEAN UP

▲ The 1972 movie *Silent Running* featured three small robots that acted as housekeepers on a futuristic spacecraft.

Robot workers are coming into the home. They are being designed to do household chores, which will save people a lot of time and work.

One of the first robot gadgets to be sold to the public was the iRobot Roomba vacuum cleaner. Roomba is a small machine that measures only a little bigger than a large dinner plate. Using the Roomba is fun. First, it is placed in the middle of the room that needs cleaning. When it is switched on, it begins to make beeping noises. The beeps indicate that sensors are checking Roomba's systems and the room.

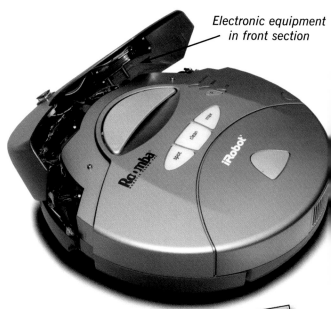

Electronic equipment in front section

▲ A "virtual wall" is created by a small projector that sends a beam across a doorway. The Roomba will not cross the beam.

ROBOFACTS: WINDOW CLEANERS

Cleaning windows is a challenging chore for a robot. To clean windows, robotic engineers and designers had to figure out how to attach robots to a vertical surface.

One kind of robot (right) hangs on to the window with three sucker pads, while the fourth pad reaches out to change the robot's position. The washing and drying equipment are carried in the body section, and cables connect the robot to a power supply on the ground.

Another robotic cleaner, designed by the German company Fraunhofer, uses two spinning suckers to skate back and forth across the glass.

Sucker pads on extending arms and legs

Power and control cables

Main power charger

Rechargeable battery

▶ The Roomba is just one type of robot made by the iRobot corporation. It was first introduced in 2002, and only three years later, more than a million had been sold. Upgrades include custom case designs to personalize its appearance to customers' tastes.

Sensor checks for edges to avoid falling down stairs

Remote control

Virtual wall projector

Drive wheels made of soft rubber for good grip on hard floors

Cleaning roller and brush system

Comb to clean jammed parts

Removable dust filter

Once Roomba has the room mapped in its computer memory, it sets off in a spiral pattern. When it bumps into a chair or table leg, the Roomba backs away and goes around it, updating its memory-map as it moves around the room.

Dust tray slides out of back for emptying

Roomba is best suited for light, household vacuuming, because it has only a small dust tray. In the future, more advanced models will be able to tackle larger tasks.

INTELLIGENT HOMES

Robots can be used to make life easier for people in their homes. They can also help make homes more evironmentally friendly.

▲ Tomy Omnibot household robots were on sale in the 1980s. This knee-high model had a remote control, an alarm clock, and could play music tapes.

Robots can do more in a home than clean. Some are being designed to help homes use less energy. Most energy comes from electricity that is made by burning **fossil fuels**, which also releases **greenhouse gases** and other pollutants. A home that uses less energy creates less pollution.

Central computers in a house can control the temperature of a house. By keeping a house at an ideal temperature, energy is not wasted. This can cut winter heating and summer cooling bills and save energy.

Central computers can also control **solar panels** and other environmentally friendly heat- and power-generating systems. This could mean that a robot-controlled home would need little or no energy from a polluting power station.

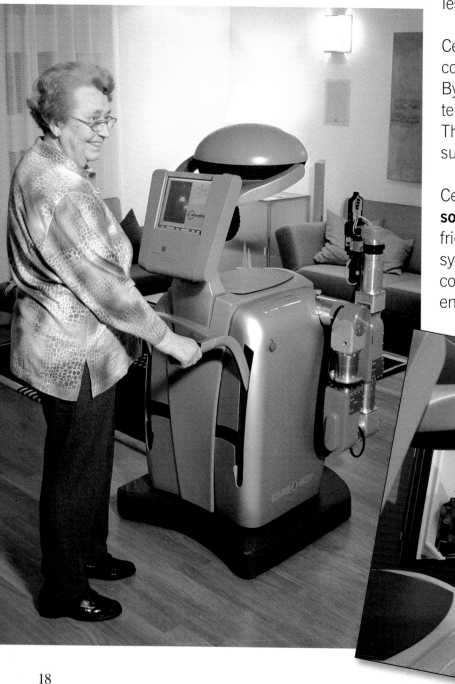

◄ The elderly can be helped by robots like the Care-O-bot. The Care-O-bot can be controlled by a keypad or by voice command. It can help with many tasks, such as getting drinks and answering the door. It can also act as a walking aid, helping a disabled person to move around safely.

This refrigerator keeps track of what is stored inside. When food gets low, it orders more through an Internet link

The Roboking is one of several robotic vacuums on sale

This robot duster crawls on tracks. It cleans air conditioning ducts to keep them free of dirt

A central computer controls all of a home's systems. It keeps the house at a comfortable temperature, and controls the security system

▶ These machines are just a few of the robots already available. It is likely that in years to come, new homes will come with a central home computer that controls different robotic systems.

Future versions of this robot maid will be slimmer, so it can move around easily in small rooms

A robot mower keeps the grass neatly trimmed

Homes controlled by robotic systems will be able to look after the people living in them. Sensors located throughout the homes will monitor how people are living. For example, sensors embedded in refrigerators can monitor what a person eats, ensuring they stick to a good diet.

Various models of human-like robots are being developed. Small models are likely to be popular since they can move around homes easily.

ROBOFACTS: SMART OFFICES

Some large buildings use robotic systems that can save energy and money. Walls with vents and shutters that open and shut automatically allow a building to release heat, so no air conditioning is needed. These systems also allow a building to become its own power station and actually make energy by collecting heat from the Sun.

The flow of air in this building is controlled by a central computer

ROBOTS EVERYWHERE

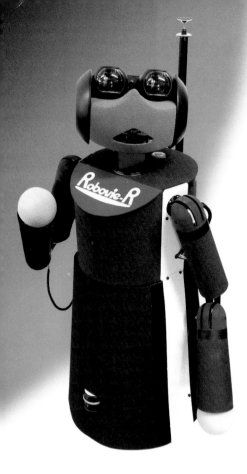

Robots are everywhere. They work in factories, homes, offices, and even museums. They have also been popular characters in movies and books.

The American company Sarcos makes robots that are meant to entertain people. Designers, artists, and craftspeople make skins and other coverings so the robots look as real as possible. Sarcos robots are controlled by remote operators wearing special suits, or by **computer programs**.

◀ Robovie-R is part of a project to make robots that will live with and communicate with humans.

Three robots work at the Communications Museum in Berlin, Germany. The Inciting (middle) welcomes visitors as they enter, the Instructor (right) leads guided tours, while the Twiddling (left) scurries about, playing with the red ball.

▼ The museum robots roll along at just over one mile per hour (1.6 kilometers per hour). They have laser scanners to avoid objects or people.

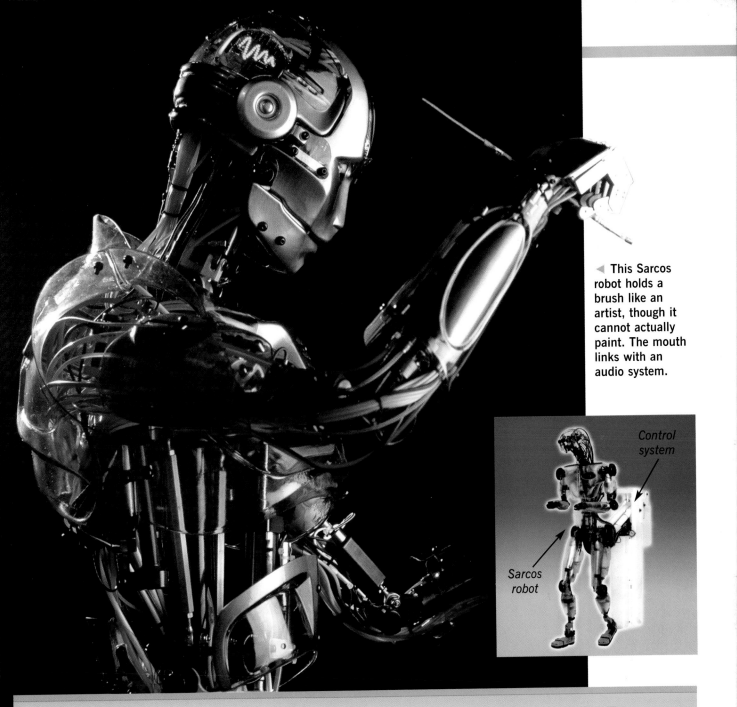

◄ This Sarcos robot holds a brush like an artist, though it cannot actually paint. The mouth links with an audio system.

Control system

Sarcos robot

ROBOFACTS: SCI-FI VISION OF A FUTURE ROBOT WORLD

Robots are often important characters in science fiction books and movies, such as *I, Robot,* a movie released in 2004.

The makers of *I, Robot* worked hard to make the robots look as real as possible, with abilities that make today's robots look very primitive.

One of the biggest differences between the robots of today and those that appear in *I, Robot* is in their movements. Today's robots can walk or climb stairs only with great care. In *I, Robot,* future robots run and leap about in a way that would make an Olympic athlete green with envy. Will that ever come true? We will have to wait and see!

One of several robot designs featured in the movie

Newly built robots line up in an assembly plant

LIFE SAVERS

Surgeons already use robotic equipment in some operations. Eventually, tiny robots may travel in our bodies to make repairs from the inside.

▲ In the future, some medical micro-robots may look like tiny submarines. Injected into arteries, they would deliver medicine to the site of injury.

The da Vinci robot helps perform surgery. A surgeon operates da Vinci while sitting at a computer **console** that shows three-dimensional images of the operation site. The surgery is performed by up to four robotic arms that are controlled by the doctor. The da Vinci robot has revolutionized surgery, because it allows surgical instruments to be inserted through small incisions no bigger than the width of a finger. Small holes are much quicker to heal than large incisions, and also minimize pain and the risk of infection.

Da Vinci's robot arm

Da Vinci's camera-view shown on video screen

Surgeon

Patient's stomach

► This robotic equipment has a probe that measures a skull and feeds the information into a computer. Using this "mapping" information, brain operations can be made simpler and safer.

ROBOFACTS: WOULD YOU LIKE A ROBODOCTOR?

RP-6 robots allow doctors to examine and talk to patients from anywhere in the world, using the Internet. The 64-inch (1.6-meter) high RP-6 rolls through hospital corridors and has a computer screen and video camera mounted on top.

A doctor guides the RP-6 using a joystick controller in the doctor's home or office. Sitting in front of a screen, the doctor can see the patient, ask questions, and read notes and x-rays, all by using the equipment carried on the RP-6. At the same time, the patient sees the doctor's face on the robot's computer screen.

The RP-6 has become a popular piece of equipment and is starting to be used by many big hospitals around the world. Doctors can also use the RP-6 to talk with other doctors, no matter what country they happen to be in.

The RP-6 has 24 sensors to help it find its way around a hospital

A medical robot from the movie *Star Wars*

BRAVEBOTS

Robots are ideal for working in dangerous places. Having robots do risky jobs means that people avoid injury or death.

▲ The Mobot moved around on a wheeled box. Two television cameras showed the operator what was in front of the robot.

The **nuclear industry** uses **radioactive** materials. These materials give off **radiation**, or invisible rays of energy, that can make people sick or die. Handling such materials is an ideal job for a robot because they are not affected by radiation.

The Mobot, built in 1960, was designed so its operator sat safely behind protective shielding, working the machine with gloves that were electronically linked to the robot. Mobot's arms and grippers copied the operator's movements exactly.

Four-wheel drive mine rescue robot

Guardrobo experimental firefighter robot

◄ ▲ Mines and fires are other danger zones for which robots are being developed.

◄ Researcher Bob Anderson checks out one of M2's video sensors at this desert base.

The M2 Mighty Mouse is a robot currently being used to safely handle deadly materials. M2 proved its worth in 2005, when it was used to free a radioactive cylinder that was trapped in a research laboratory. Mighty Mouse can work in an area filled with enough radiation to kill 40 people.

◄ Manny is a robot used to test space suits, firefighting gear, and clothes used to survive in hazardous environments, such as places where there are leaks of poison gas or dangerous chemicals.

Manny moves like a person and has systems that simulate sweating and breathing, allowing the robot to imitate how a person would react in the clothing.

This Russian Navy robot was built for underwater repair work

ROBOFACTS:
UNDERWATER WORKERS

Remote-operated vehicles, or ROVs, are underwater robots that do many jobs once done by divers, especially deep sea work which is dangerous for people.

Mining robot sucks mineral-bearing rocks from the sea floor

Working an ROV is like playing a video game. The operator sits aboard a ship, watching the action on a television. Several screens show data from the ROV as well as views from different cameras. The ROV's movements are controlled using a video game-style joystick and keyboard.

ROVs are vital for submarine rescues as well as checking on oil rigs and their pipe systems.

THINGS TO COME?

Robots are here to stay, and future robot workers will be capable of more advanced tasks than those of today.

▲ More powerful computers may allow advanced robots to work at important jobs, such as school crossing guards.

Future industrial robots will be more powerful, able to do more complex jobs, and be made of lighter and stronger materials.

▲ Robots at work spraying vehicle bodies with paint.

Improvements in robot design can come in other ways too. For example, a robot that sprays paint on vehicles wastes less of the paint because it uses a cartridge for painting, instead of long tubes. When there is a color change, only the paint cartridge needs to be swapped. There are no tubes to be disconnected, emptied, and cleaned between different shades.

ROBOFACTS: BRAIN-SCAN CONTROL

Brain scanning machine, with fingers in the white circle

Scan data used by computer

In the future, robots could be controlled by human brain waves.

In 2006, robots were used in experiments in which a person was put in a brain-scanning machine, normally used by medical staff in hospitals. The person made a hand gesture, such as the two-finger "V" sign. The brain wave created when the gesture was made was detected by the scanning machine and sent to a computer.

A computer program analyzed the brain wave and sent the results to a robotic hand. The hand then made the same hand gesture as the person.

Currently, there are some drawbacks. There is a seven-second delay while the computer analyzes the brain pattern, and it is accurate only about 85 percent of the time, which is not reliable enough for use in the real world. The research team believes the technology could be in wide use within ten years.

Robot hand repeats the same gesture as man in brain scanner

BRAIN
Constant improvements in the processing power of computers means that robots are becoming more capable and more "intelligent." This will allow robots to do many more jobs than they are capable of today.

SENSES
Improvements with sensors will allow robots to recognize objects quicker and with more reliability. Robots will also be able to tell people apart easily by analyzing their appearances or voices. This is possible now, but it is not reliable.

CONTROL
Improved communication technology will speed up robot reflexes. Light beams may replace today's radio signals in some cases, as these can carry much more information. Many robots will be linked to the Internet, which will be used to update their memories with new material when available.

POWER
New kinds of batteries, such as hydrogen fuel cells, will enable robots to operate for longer periods of time. Recharging will also be quicker, as fuel cells can be filled up with hydrogen fuel in a few moments.

STRUCTURE
Robots will be made of lightweight materials, based on ceramics and super strong plastics. Robots that are lighter use less battery power, allowing them to work longer before they need to be recharged.

MUSCLES
Light weight and more power from improved batteries means that future robots will be agile, or able to move quickly and nimbly.

▲ The next generation of robots will be built using advanced technologies that are still being developed by research teams.

Advances in computer technology will make big differences to robotics. With more processing power, which is the speed robots analyze data in their computer "brains," robots will be able to carry out more complex jobs. Simple actions we take for granted, such as running or handling objects, will become easier for robots, too.

TIME TRACK

▲ The PUMA industrial arm was developed in 1978. This type of arm has become one of the most popular types in use.

Here are some of the events and machines covering the story of automation **and robotics.**

▲ An industrial robot checks the paint finish on a vehicle body.

1920 The word "robot" is used for the first time when Czech writer Karel Capek writes a stage play about robots trying to take over the world. The word was coined by Capek's brother, from the Czech word "robota," meaning "work."

1943 Science fiction writer Isaac Asimov coins the word "robotics" to describe the technology of robots. Through his series of stories based on a robot theme, he predicts the rise of a powerful future robotics industry.

1943 ENIAC, or Electronic Numerical Integrator And Computer, is the world's first electronic computer that runs from a program.

1954 George Devol and Joseph Engelberger develop the first programmable robot in 1954, and two years later start Unimation Inc., the first company to make robot arms. Five years of effort results in their first industrial robot, the Unimate.

1961 The first industrial robot goes to work at a General Motors car plant in the United States. The Unimate picks up hot pieces of metal and places them in neat stacks.

1968 The first miniaturized computer circuit on a chip of silicon is perfected. The "microchip" becomes the basis of all computing machines made since, including robots.

1968 Kawasaki of Japan buys a license to build robots from Unimation and starts making them successfully. In 1986, Kawasaki starts to build its own robot designs.

1969 The Stanford Arm is perfected by robotics engineer Victor Scheinman. The electric-powered Arm has six degrees of freedom, allowing it to reach any point in its workspace. The Stanford Arm opens the way to more advanced robots that can do such things as assembling and welding. In 1977, Scheinman sells his design to Unimation Inc.

1973 KUKA Robotics builds an industrial robot called Famulus. It is the first such robot to have six degrees of freedom.

1973 The Cincinnati Milacron company introduces the T3, "The Tomorrow Tool." It is the first commercially available industrial robot controlled by a microcomputer.

▲ A complex array of microchip circuits lies at the heart of all robotic control systems.

1978   The Unimation robot company develops the Stanford Arm as the PUMA, or Programmable Universal Machine for Assembly.

1970s   Computers start to come into general use, using microchip technology. They are followed by desktop models in the 1980s. In many countries, they are now in almost every office, school, and home.

1970s   Interest in industrial robots grows and many companies start making them, especially in Japan. By 2000, Japanese companies are world leaders in robotics.

1986   Honda of Japan starts to develop robots, with E0 the first in a series. The 287-pound (130-kilogram) P3 model of 1997 is the first human-like robot to walk under its own power. By 2005, Honda has created the smaller and lighter Asimo model, which can talk, walk, and climb stairs.

1995   The Intuitive Surgical company is formed to design and sell advanced surgical robotic systems. In 1999, the da Vinci robot is introduced. By 2006, the da Vinci system has been installed in more than 300 hospitals.

2000   About 100,000 new industrial robots are manufactured and installed worldwide during the year. Nearly half of these are in Japan, which is by far the world's biggest user of robots.

2000   A Canadian-built robotic arm, the SSRMS, or Space Station Remote Manipulator System, is launched into space to work on assembly of the International Space Station. Canadian robotic arms have also been used on American space shuttles.

2002   The world's population of industrial robots reaches nearly 800,000. By 2004, this has risen to about 1 million.

2002   The iRobot Corporation introduces its Roomba cleaner. By 2006, sales of the robot home helper have passed the 2 million mark.

2004   The movie *I, Robot* is released. It is a science fiction action-adventure, based around the ideas of American writer and scientist Isaac Asimov.

2006   Honda experiments with brain-scanning equipment that can command a robot hand to repeat human hand gestures.

2010-2015   New homes and vehicles may be fitted with robotic systems. These systems could run households, from daily cleaning work to operating a burglar alarm.

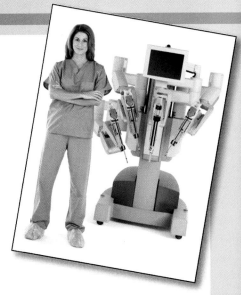

▲ **The da Vinci robotic surgery system has helped to save many lives since its introduction in 1999.**

▲ **The 1999 P3 robot (right) with the newer and smaller Asimo model.**

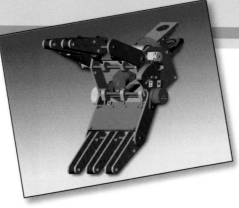

▶ **End effectors are the parts that do the actual work. Here is a robotic hand with finger-like grippers.**

GLOSSARY

Here are explanations of many technical terms in this book.

Antenna Any aerial that is used to send or receive radio or television signals. Antennas come in many shapes and sizes. Most are slim rods or round dish shapes.

Artery A tube that carries blood from the heart to other organs and tissues in the body.

Automated When machines do the work instead of people.

Brain wave Electrical signal made by the brain, which scientists can record and measure.

Circuit Any electronic linkage that joins two or more parts together.

Computer program The set of instructions that are fed into a computer to make it work. A program is used for each separate job – for a robot, this might be a pick and place program or one for pattern recognition. "Software" is another word used generally for programs.

Console A panel that houses controls for mechanical or electronic equipment.

Data Information that is sent or received by any electronic or robotic system. Data may be in the form of a program or as various forms of feedback from sensors.

DOF Degrees of Freedom. Describes the various ways in which a robot arm can move, in roll, pitch, and yaw. Movements can also be described in axes – x-axis (side to side), y-axis (front to back), and z-axis (up and down).

Fossil fuels A fuel that is found underground, such as oil, coal, or natural gas.

Fuel cell A type of battery in which output is continuous, so long as a fuel is passed through it. Most fuel cells use hydrogen gas or liquid. This is a very clean fuel, and the only waste is pure water.

GPS Global Positioning System. GPS satellites circling the Earth send out radio signals that allow anyone on the ground with a receiver to know their position and altitude to within a few meters.

Greenhouse gas A gas, such as carbon dioxide, that gets trapped in the atmosphere. Greenhouse gases trap the Sun's heat in the atmosphere and cause temperatures to increase.

Intelligence In robotics, a term that describes a smart machine able to do a task that would need thinking about if done by a human. It is usually known as "AI", for Artificial Intelligence.

Ladar LAser Detection And Ranging. A system that uses a laser beam, which is an extremely narrow beam of intense light, to map its surroundings. Ladar works by sending out a beam, then measuring the time and position of laser light reflected from objects that are in its path.

Microchip The tiny, calculating part of any computer or robotic device. Microchips have taken the wires and cables of old-fashioned electronics and reduced them in size by printing them as a circuit pattern on a small slice of silicon, known as a "chip." A computer based on microchip technology is called a microcomputer.

Nuclear industry An industry that deals with nuclear energy. Nuclear energy does not create greenhouse gases but it does create waste that can be harmful to people and the environment if not stored properly.

Radiation Any form of energy given out, such as light, heat, radio waves, or television signals. Nuclear power stations work by using radioactive materials to heat water for steam turbines. So long as they are well shielded by thick concrete, these materials are usually safe. If a human is exposed for more than a very short time, the radiation damages living cells, resulting in disease or death.

Radioactive A substance that emits radiation.

Ram A mechanical part that drives other parts by exerting pressure on them.

Solar panel A flat panel that converts the energy in light to electricity. Passive solar panels can be used to heat water by absorbing the heat in sunlight.

Welding Joining together pieces of metal by heating them to a high temperature.

Workspace The volume of space in which a robotic arm can reach and perform its functions.

X-ray Radiation that passes through soft materials, such as human flesh. X-rays are used in hospitals to take pictures of bones. The bones are solid, so the x-rays do not pass through them.

▲ A few of the da Vinci robot's surgical instruments. They are shown here with a coin to show their small size.

▶ Some of the many kinds of build-up kits that are made for robot enthusiasts.

ROBOZONES: NEXT STEPS

Robotics is an interesting area of science, and one that is making advances quickly. There are a lot of ways to get involved, including looking at what is available in hobby stores.

The best robots are those that you can program yourself. Lego Mindstorms kits are a good place to start. These kits allow you to build robotic toy vehicles and other robotic devices.

Electronic stores and Internet sites sell a range of robot products, from basic robot parts to the simple self-assembly robot kits that are shown at right.

Using this kind of equipment, either to build something completely from scratch, or as an add-on to an existing robot, is a great way to learn about robotics.

INDEX

Acknowledgements
We wish to thank all those individuals and organizations that have helped to create this publication. Information and images were supplied by:
ABB, Alio Industries, Alpha Archive, ATR Intelligent Robotics and Communication Laboratories, BMW AG, Cincinnati Milacron, DARPA, FANUC Robotics, Fraunhofer IPA, FU Berlin, Peter Galbraith, Hitachi Corp, Honda Motor Co, Intuitive Surgical Inc, IS Robotics, iStockphoto, David Jefferis, Kokoro Dreams, KUKA Roboter GmbH, LG Electronics, Peter Menzel, MIT AI Lab, Mitsubishi Electric Corp, NASA, NEC Corp, Gavin Page/Design Shop, Philippe Psaila, Ransomes Jacobsen Ltd, Robotics Research Corp, Sandia National Laboratories, Sanger Centre, Kiyoshi Takahase Segundo/Fotolia, Science Photo Library, Shadow Robot Company, Sony Corp, Ben Spinler, Staubli Group, Stellex Precision Machine Inc, Stephen Sweet, Wincor Nixdorf GmbH & Co. KG

Printed in the U.S.A.